LITERACY BOOK

English
No Problem!

Reproducible
Masters

Elizabeth Minicz
William Rainey Harper College
Palatine, IL

Marcia L. Taylor
Bernard Kleiman JobLink Learning Center
ISPAT Inland Steel, Inc.
East Chicago, IN

Vision Literacy
540 Valley Way
Milpitas, CA 95035

New Readers Press

English—No Problem!™
English—No Problem! Literacy Reproducible Masters
ISBN 1-56420-365-4

Copyright © 2004 New Readers Press
New Readers Press
Division of ProLiteracy Worldwide
1320 Jamesville Avenue, Syracuse, New York 13210
www.newreaderspress.com

All rights reserved. No part of this book may be reproduced or transmitted in any form or by any means, electronic or mechanical, including photocopying, recording, or by any information storage and retrieval system, without permission in writing from the publisher.

Printed in the United States of America
9 8 7 6 5 4 3 2

All proceeds from the sale of New Readers Press materials support literacy programs in the United States and worldwide.

Acquisitions Editor: Paula L. Schlusberg
Developer: Mendoza and Associates
Project Director: Roseanne Mendoza
Project Editor: Pat Harrington-Wydell
Content Editor: Terrie Lipke
Production Director: Heather Witt-Badoud
Designer: Kimbrly Koennecke
Illustrations: Janet Ohlsen, James Wallace
Production Specialist: Jeffrey R. Smith
Cover Design: Kimbrly Koennecke
Cover Photography: Robert Mescavage Photography

Contents

Teacher Directions for Unit Checkup/Review 5

Reproducible Masters

Customizable Graphic Organizers

Master 1	Bingo Chart
Master 2	2-Column Chart
Master 3	3-Column Chart
Master 4	4-Column Chart
Master 5	Idea Map
Master 6	Calendar

Generic Assessment Masters

Master 7	Oral Communication Rubric
Master 8	Written Communication Rubric

Masters for Warm-Up Unit A

Master 9	Reading: Letters and Numbers – **Use after Lesson 5, page 15.**
Master 10	Game: Go Fish – **Use after Lesson 5, page 15.**

Masters for Warm-Up Unit B

Master 11	Reading: Find the Letter – **Use after Lesson 5, page 21.**
Master 12	Game: Going to School – **Use after Lesson 5, page 21.**
Master 13	Game: What Color Is It? – **Use after Lesson 5, page 21.**

Masters for Unit 1

Master 14	Reading: The Letter *P* – **Use after Lesson 1, page 26.**
Master 15	Study Skills: Follow Directions – **Use after Lesson 1, page 26.**
Master 16	Game: Is This My Classroom? – **Use after Lesson 2, page 29.**
Master 17	Unit Checkup/Review – **Use to assess or review Unit 1. Has two pages.**

Masters for Unit 2

Master 18	Life Skills: Who Are You? – **Use after Lesson 1, page 35.**
Master 19	Reading: The Letter *M* – **Use after Lesson 2, page 40.**
Master 20	Reading: The Letter *N* – **Use after Lesson 2, page 40.**
Master 21	Game: Tell Me the Answer – **Use after Lesson 2, page 40.**
Master 22	Unit Checkup/Review – **Use to assess or review Unit 2. Has two pages.**

English—No Problem! **Literacy 3**

Masters for Unit 3

Master 23   Game: Make a Face – **Use after Lesson 1, page 45.**
Master 24   Reading: The Letter B – **Use after Lesson 2, page 47.**
Master 25   Reading: The Letter D – **Use after Lesson 2, page 48.**
Master 26   Life Skills: Using Polite Language – **Use after Lesson 2, page 50.**
Master 27   Unit 3 Project: Your Week – **Use with the Unit 3 Project, page 51.**
Master 28   Unit Checkup/Review – **Use to assess or review Unit 3. Has two pages.**

Masters for Unit 4

Master 29   Game: Spend! Spend! Spend! – **Use after Lesson 1, page 55.**
Master 30   Reading: The Letter T – **Use after Lesson 1, page 56.**
Master 31   Reading: Months – **Use after Lesson 2, page 58.**
Master 32   Life Skills: Writing a Check – **Use after Lesson 2, page 59.**
Master 33   Reading: The Letter F – **Use after Lesson 2, page 60.**
Master 34   Unit 4 Project: Places You Pay Cash – **Use with the Unit 4 Project, page 61.**
Master 35   Unit Checkup/Review – **Use to assess or review Unit 4. Has two pages.**

Masters for Unit 5

Master 36   Life Skills: Organize Information – **Use after Lesson 1, page 65.**
Master 37   Reading: The Letter H – **Use after Lesson 1, page 65.**
Master 38   Game: Match the Facts – **Use after Lesson 2, page 68.**
Master 39   Reading: The Letter L – **Use after Lesson 2, page 70.**
Master 40   Unit 5 Project: Going Shopping – **Use with the Unit 5 Project, page 71.**
Master 41   Unit Checkup/Review – **Use to assess or review Unit 5. Has two pages.**

Masters for Unit 6

Master 42   Reading: The Letter S – **Use after Lesson 2, page 79.**
Master 43   Reading: The Letter R – **Use after Lesson 2, page 79.**
Master 44   Life Skills: Organize Information – **Use after Lesson 2, page 79.**
Master 45   Game: Match the Words – **Use after Lesson 2, page 79.**
Master 46   Unit 6 Project: Make a Class Map – **Use with the Unit 6 Project, page 81.**
Master 47   Unit Checkup/Review – **Use to assess or review Unit 6. Has two pages.**

Answers and Listening Scripts 59

Teacher Directions for Unit Checkup/Review
(Unit Masters 17, 22, 28, 35, 41, 47)

Unit Checkups are designed to be scored on a scale of 100 points. These points are divided among the four parts. Suggested point values for specific questions are given in Answers and Listening Scripts in the back of this book. If a learner scores below 70 points on a Unit Checkup, have him or her review the material and take the Unit Checkup again. If a learner has trouble with only some parts of a Unit Checkup, you can have the learner review for and retake just those parts.

Master 1

Name: _____ Date: _____ Class: _____

Customizable Graphic Organizer
Bingo Chart

_____

1	2	3	4	5

English—No Problem! **Literacy**

Master 2

Name: _____ Date: _____ Class: _____

Customizable Graphic Organizer
2–Column Chart

_____

English—No Problem! **Literacy**

Master 3

Name:_____ Date:_____ Class:_____

Customizable Graphic Organizer
3–Column Chart

_____

English—No Problem! **Literacy**

Master 4

Name:_____ Date:_____ Class:_____

Customizable Graphic Organizer
4–Column Chart

_____

English—No Problem! **Literacy**

Master 5

Name: _____ Date: _____ Class: _____

Customizable Graphic Organizer
Idea Map

English—No Problem! **Literacy**

Master 6

Name: _____ Date: _____ Class: _____

Customizable Graphic Organizer
Calendar

English—No Problem! **Literacy**

Master 7

Name: _____ Date: _____ Class: _____

Generic Assessment Master
Oral Communication Rubric

How are your learners progressing? Use this set of rubrics to track progress as your learners engage in discussions, dialogues, and presentations.

Category	1	2	3	4
Fluency	No fluency; can only repeat words stated by others or recite memorized words and phrases	Speaks in isolated words and formulaic phrases in between long gaps	Speech is mostly formulaic but can sometimes be spontaneous, with frequent pauses and rephrasing	Can produce spontaneous speech, but hesitant, with silences to search for the correct word
Accuracy	No knowledge of grammar; cannot use accurate forms apart from memorized phrases	Can use several basic forms; no accuracy when speaking beyond these features	Some control of very basic grammar in speaking; frequent errors	Controls some complex forms; frequent errors in grammar that occasionally obscure meaning
Pronunciation	Heavily influenced by the first language and often unintelligible	Often influenced by the first language and frequently difficult to understand	Somewhat clear at times, but frequently causes misunderstanding and rephrasing	Clear for a number of statements, with a strong, noticeable accent
Vocabulary	No command of vocabulary in speech beyond repeating the words of others	Vocabulary limited to a few isolated words and phrases	Vocabulary centers on basic objects, places, and common family terms	Uses some complex words and a range of basic vocabulary; often uses the wrong word
Appropriateness (accuracy and politeness with language functions)	No functional communicative ability beyond a few simple phrases such as "thank you"	Asks and responds to very simple learned questions; can deal with survival needs	Can participate in very basic conversations in a few routine social situations	Uses some formulaic expressions correctly, but could be seen as too blunt in some situations

Total Score: _____

English—No Problem! Literacy

Master 8

Name:_____ Date:_____ Class:_____

Generic Assessment Master
Written Communication Rubric

How are your students progressing? Use this set of rubrics to track progress as the students engage in various forms of writing to complete tasks and projects.

Category	1	2	3	4
Content	Copies the letters of the alphabet, numbers, and basic personal information	Can write a limited number of very common words and basic personal information on simplified forms	Can write common words and phrases related to immediate needs such as taking telephone messages and creating questions	Can perform basic writing tasks such as short personal notes and letters, using statements, questions, and a range of personal vocabulary
Organization	Word-level; writes individual words in lists with no organizational pattern	Phrase-level; can follow structure of simplified form or application, using common words and phrases	Sentence-level; can produce a series of simple sentences related to a topic	Simple discourse level; can follow the basic organization for letters and notes
Mechanics	No use of punctuation or capitalization	Capitalizes some proper nouns; no use of punctuation	Capitalizes proper nouns and the beginnings of sentences; uses periods to end sentences	Capitalizes words consistently; uses periods, commas, and other punctuation with frequent errors
Language Use	No command of grammar beyond copying the words of others	Able to write simple fixed expressions; cannot write grammatically without assistance	Able to write simple grammatical sentences, but with frequent errors; needs assistance	Able to write some simple sentences without errors, but often makes errors

Total Score: _____

English—No Problem! Literacy

Master 9 Use after Lesson 5, page 15.

Name: _____ Date: _____ Class: _____

Warm-Up Unit A: Cecile's Day
Reading: Letters and Numbers

Speak. Listen. Write.

Partner A speaks.
C6: H
D7: S
C8: T
D5: T
C7: A
D8: K
C5: C
D6: A

Partner A writes.

	1	2	3	4
A				
B				

Partner B writes.

	5	6	7	8
C				
D				

fold here

Partner B speaks.
A2: E
B3: P
A4: D
B1: C
A3: A
B4: Y
A1: R
B2: O

English—No Problem! Literacy

Master 10 Use after Lesson 5, page 15.

Name _____ Date: _____ Class: _____

Warm-Up Unit A: Cecile's Day
Game: Go Fish

A	F	K	P	U	Z
B	G	L	Q	V	
C	H	M	R	W	
D	I	N	S	X	
E	J	O	T	Y	

To the Teacher: Copy this page four times and then cut out cards along dotted lines.

English—No Problem! **Literacy**

Master 11 Use after Lesson 5, page 21.

Name: _____ Date: _____ Class: _____

Warm-Up Unit B: Omar's Day
Reading: Find the Letter

Partner A speaks.
1. Circle a.
2. Circle e.
3. Circle h.
4. Circle o.
5. Circle f.
6. Circle m.
7. Circle s.
8. Circle y.

Partner B follows directions.
1. d(a)y
2. C e c i l e
3. a l p h a b e t
4. p a r k i n g   l o t
5. o f f i c e
6. h o m e
7. l i s t e n
8. p h a r m a c y

Partner A follows directions.
1. s(c)h o o l
2. r e a d
3. v i d e o
4. s t o r e
5. w h i t e
6. o r a n g e
7. e i g h t
8. z e r o

Partner B speaks.
1. Circle c.
2. Circle e.
3. Circle i.
4. Circle r.
5. Circle t.
6. Circle g.
7. Circle h.
8. Circle z.

English—No Problem! **Literacy**

Master 12   Use after Lesson 5, page 21.

Name:_____ Date:_____ Class:_____

Warm-Up Unit B: Omar's Day
Game: Going to School

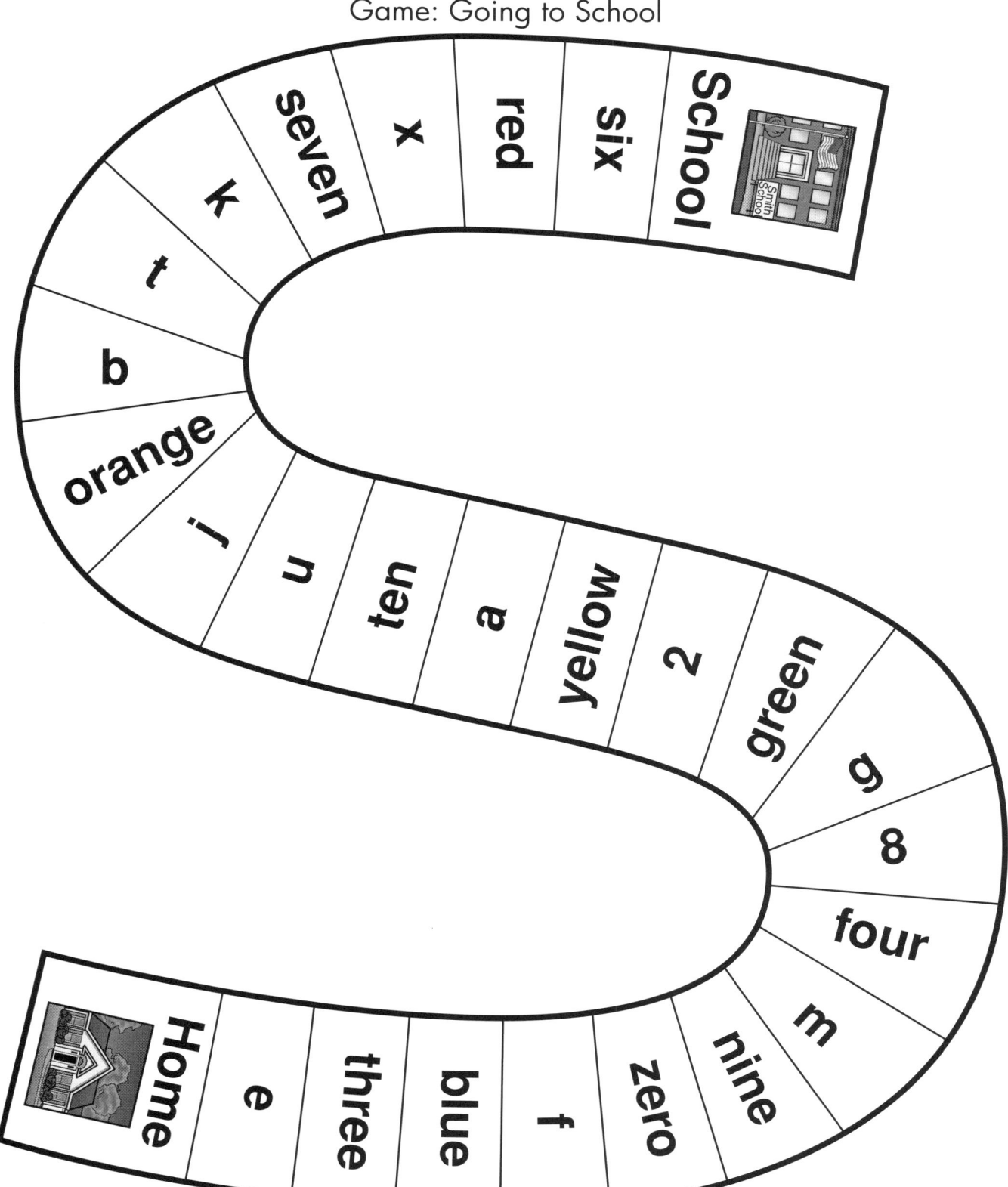

Master 13   Use after Lesson 5, page 21.

Name: _____ Date: _____ Class: _____

Warm-Up Unit B: Omar's Day
Game: What Color Is It?

Listen and color the boxes.

Partner A speaks.
- J5: yellow
- L4: red
- K3: white
- J4: brown
- K4: blue
- L5: orange
- J3: green
- K5: black
- L3: purple

fold here

Partner B colors.

	3	4	5
J			
K			
L			

Partner A colors.

	8	9	10
T			
U			
V			

Partner B speaks.
- T8: blue
- U9: white
- V8: black
- U8: yellow
- V10: purple
- T9: red
- V9: brown
- T10: green
- U10: orange

English—No Problem! Literacy

Master 14 Use after Lesson 1, page 26.

Name:_____ Date:_____ Class:_____

Unit 1: Welcome!
Reading: The Letter P

A. Copy *P* and *p*.

P P ____ ____ ____ ____

p p ____ ____ ____ ____

B. Listen and write.

pen	*p*en	*pen*
pencil	__encil	_____
point	__oint	_____
purple	__urple	_____
repeat	re__eat	_____

C. Write more words with *p*.

_____ _____ _____

_____ _____ _____

Show the words to your teacher.
Show the words to a classmate.

English—No Problem! **Literacy**

Master 15 Use after Lesson 1, page 26.

Name: _____ Date: _____ Class: _____

Unit 1: Welcome!
Study Skills: Follow Directions

A. Listen and write the number.

point	learn	listen	check
___	___	___	_1_

speak	read	write	repeat
___	___	___	___

B. Listen and write the number.

teacher	student	pen	classroom
___	___	___	___

notebook	home	pencil	book
_12_	___	___	___

English—No Problem! Literacy

Master 16   Use after Lesson 2, page 29.

Name: _____ Date: _____ Class: _____

Unit 1: Welcome!
Game: Is This My Classroom?

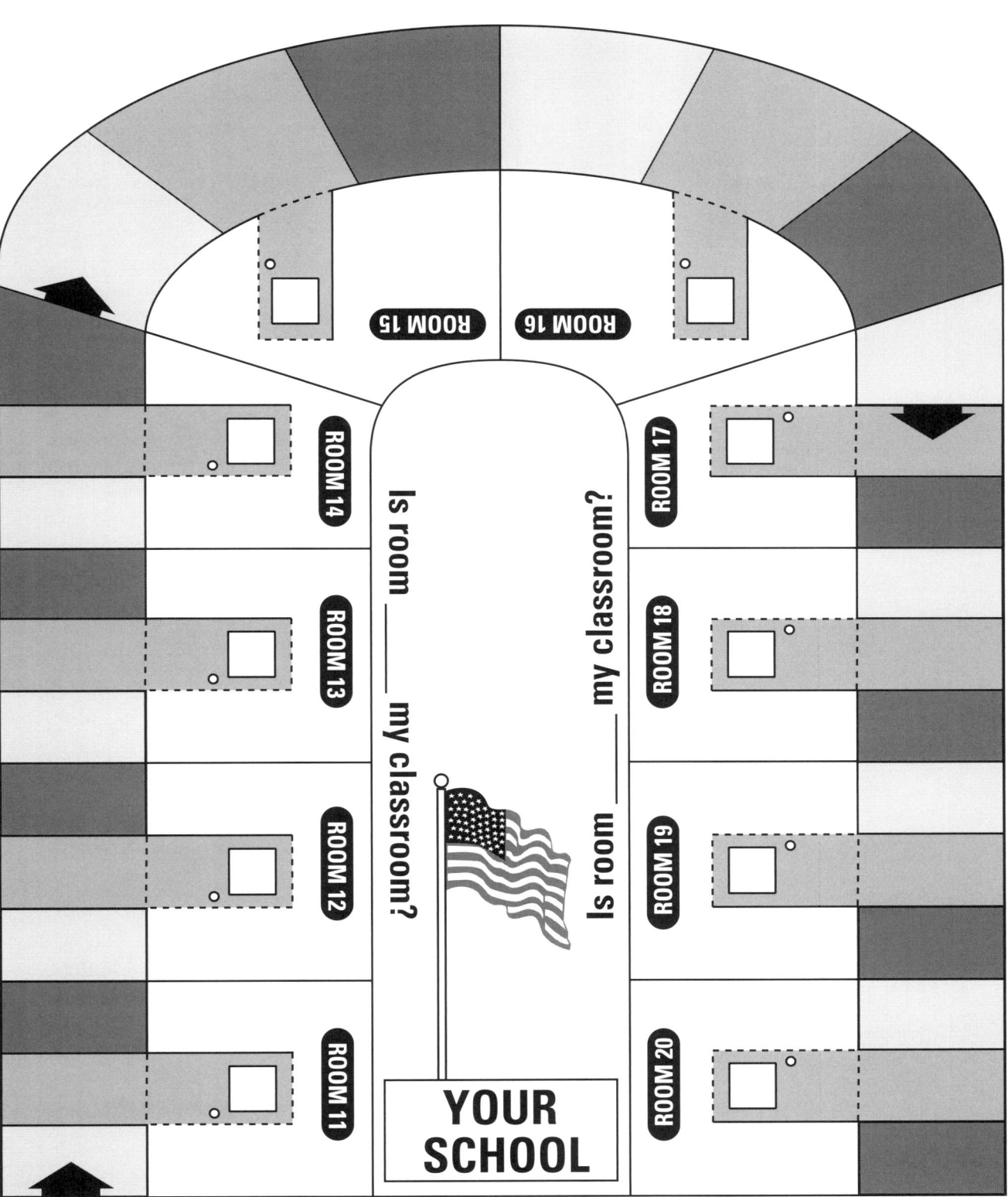

Start Here

English—No Problem! Literacy

Master 17a Use to assess or review Unit 1.

Name: _____ Date: _____ Class: _____

Unit 1: Welcome!
Unit Checkup/Review

Part 1: Learning for Life

Write your name.

1. Name: ____<u>Helen</u>_____ ____<u>Marie</u>_____ ____<u>Jankowski</u>_____
          first   middle   last

2. Name: _____ _____ _____
          first   middle   last

3. Name: _____ _____ _____
          last   first   middle

Write the number.

```
Marina Yazvec                                        655
1912 W. Blue St.
Oak Forest, IL 60025       Date  Oct. 25, 2005

PAY TO THE
ORDER OF   Oak Forest Gazette              $ 14.00

Fourteen and 00/100                                  DOLLARS

≡ First Bank  Chicago, Illinois 60670

MEMO _____  _____
⑈221271346⑈ 4672 926772⑈ 0655
```

4. $14.00 <u>fourteen and 00/100</u> Dollars
5. $12.00 _____ Dollars
6. $11.00 _____ Dollars
7. $16.00 _____ Dollars

English—No Problem! Literacy

Master 17b

Name: _____ Date: _____ Class: _____

Part 2: Listening
Listen. Circle.

1. ten pens   (eleven pencils)   a pencil   eleven people
2. an office   home   ten offices   open
3. learn   look   listen   English
4. read   home   repeat   write
5. classroom   circle   check   look
6. four books   fourteen notebooks   fourteen books   four students

Part 3: Language
Circle the word.

1. (notebook)   2. pen   3. school   4. notebook   5. teacher
   notebooks   pens   schools   notebooks   teachers

Part 4: Vocabulary

1. Write <u>pencil</u>.   _pencil_
2. Write <u>speak</u>.   _____
3. Check <u>read</u>.   read ❑   write ❑   speak ❑
4. Circle <u>school</u>.   student   study   school
5. Write <u>listen</u>.   _____
6. Check <u>office</u>.   off ❑   school ❑   office ❑
7. Circle <u>classroom</u>. room   class   classroom

English—No Problem! **Literacy**

Master 18   Use after Lesson 1, page 35.

Name:_____ Date:_____ Class:_____

Unit 2: Smile!
Life Skills: Who Are You?

Cut out the sentences. Sort into two piles: YES or NO for you.
Read the YES sentences to a partner.

I am a man.	I am a brother.
I am a male.	I am a son.
I am a female.	I am a daughter.
I am a woman.	I am a grandmother.
I am a wife.	I am a grandfather.
I am a husband.	I am a Miss.
I am a child.	I am a Mr.
I am single.	I am a Mrs.
I am married.	I am a Ms.
I am a sister.	

English—No Problem! Literacy

Master 19   Use after Lesson 2, page 40.

Name:_____   Date:_____   Class:_____

Unit 2: Smile!
Reading: The Letter M

A. Copy *M* and *m*.

M M ____

m m ____

B. Listen and write.

man   __an   _____

married   __arried   _____

mother   __other   _____

Mrs.   __rs.   _____

Mr.   __r.   _____

Miss   __iss   _____

C. Write more words with *m*. Copy the words.

1. fe_m_ale   ____female____
2. grand__other   _____
3. __s.   _____
4. __y   _____
5. wo__an   _____
6. fa__ily   _____
7. nu__ber   _____
8. e-__ail   _____

English—No Problem! **Literacy**

Master 20   Use after Lesson 2, page 40.

Name: _____ Date: _____ Class: _____

Unit 2: Smile!
Reading: The Letter N

A. Copy N and n.

N   N̤   ____

n   n̤   ____

B. Listen and write.

no   __o   _____

name   __ame   _____

nine   __ine   _____

number   __umber   _____

notebook   __otebook   _____

Nick   __ick   _____

C. Write more words with *n*. Copy the words.

1. woma**n**   _____woman_____

2. ma__   _____

3. pe__   _____

4. lear__   _____

5. so__   _____

6. liste__   _____

7. pe__cil   _____

8. stude__t   _____

English—No Problem! Literacy

Master 21 Use after Lesson 2, page 40.

Name: _____ Date: _____ Class: _____

Unit 2: Smile!
Game: Tell Me the Answer

START / FINISH	First Name	Last Name	Address	Mother's Name
State				MOVE 1 SPACE
Father's Name		Tell Me The Answer.		Zip Code
Teacher's Name				Phone Number
MOVE 1 SPACE				MOVE 1 SPACE
City				Sister's Name
Area Code	MOVE 1 SPACE	Grandfather's Name	Grandmother's Name	Brother's Name

English—No Problem! **Literacy**

Master 22a Use to assess or review Unit 2.

Name: _____ Date: _____ Class: _____

Unit 2: Smile!
Unit Checkup/Review

Part 1: Learning for Life

Lee Park
2592 Purple St.
Chicago, IL
60126
(773) 555-9287

ID: 42-09-7-18
LPark@Green.com

Write.

1. Name   _Lee Park_ _____
2. ID number   _____
3. street address _____
4. zip code   _____
5. phone number _____
6. state   _____

Part 2: Listening

Listen. Circle.

1. (mother)   father   brother
2. sister   daughter   mother
3. man   husband   son
4. wife   woman   sister
5. grandmother   grandfather   grandson
6. grandson   granddaughter   grandfather

English—No Problem! **Literacy**

GO ON

Master 22b

Name:_____ Date:_____ Class:_____

Part 3: Language
Write.

✔ I	he	she	they	you

1.  __I__

2.  _____

3.  _____

4.  _____

5.  _____

Part 4: Vocabulary
Write the number.

1. twenty-five __25__
2. twenty-two _____
3. thirty _____
4. twenty-eight _____

Read. Circle. Copy.

5. She is a father / (mother)   __She is a mother._____

6. He / She is a husband.   _____

7. She is a daughter / son.   _____

8. He / They are women.   _____

English—No Problem! **Literacy**

Master 23 Use after Lesson 1, page 45.

Name: _____ Date: _____ Class: _____

Unit 3: You're Sick
Game: Make a Face

Talk to a partner. Ask and answer questions.

Example:

English—No Problem! Literacy

Master 24   Use after Lesson 2, page 47.

Name:_____   Date:_____   Class:_____

Unit 3: You're Sick
Reading: The Letter B

A. Copy *B* and *b*.

B   B   _____
b   b   _____

B. Listen and write.

back	__ack	_____
backache	__ackache	_____
boss	__oss	_____
boy	__oy	_____
book	__ook	_____
blue	__lue	_____

C. Look for *b*. Circle the *b*. Copy the word.

note(b)ook   ___notebook___

n u m b e r   _____

h u s b a n d   _____

D. Write more words with *b*.

_____   _____

_____   _____

Show the words to your teacher.
Show the words to a classmate.

English—No Problem! **Literacy**

Master 25 Use after Lesson 2, page 48.

Name: _____ Date: _____ Class: _____

Unit 3: You're Sick
Reading: The Letter D

A. Copy D and d.

D D ____
d d ____

B. Listen and write.

Dyna   __yna   _____

day   __ay   _____

do   __o   _____

door   __oor   _____

daughter __aughter _____

C. Look for d. Circle the d. Copy the word.

Thurs(d)ay   _Thursday_

red   _____

calendar   _____

D. Write more words with d.

_____ _____

_____ _____

Show the words to your teacher.
Show the words to a classmate.

English—No Problem! Literacy

Master 26   Use after Lesson 2, page 50.

Name:_____ Date:_____ Class:_____

Unit 3: You're Sick
Life Skills: Using Polite Language

Read the sentences with a partner. Put the sentences in order.
Read the dialogues with a partner.

Dialogue A	Dialogue B
Could you repeat that?	Excuse me. Tuesday?
He has a stomachache.	I can't go to work Thursday.
Your son is sick.	No. Thursday.
A stomachache. He has a stomachache.	Oh. OK. See you Friday.
What's wrong?	

English—No Problem! **Literacy**

Master 27   Use with the Unit 3 Project, page 51.

Name: _____   Date: _____   Class: _____

Unit 3: You're Sick!
Unit 3 Project: Your Week

Write your activities for the week.

The week of: _____

Sunday	
Monday	
Tuesday	
Wednesday	
Thursday	
Friday	
Saturday	

Finished? Show your page to the class. Talk about your week.

English—No Problem!   **Literacy**

Master 28a Use to assess or review Unit 3.

Name:_____ Date:_____ Class:_____

Unit 3: You're Sick!
Unit Checkup/Review

Part 1: Learning for Life
Write the time.

1. __It's 6:30.__

3. _____

2. _____

4. _____

Read the calendar. Write the day.

| 5. Monday | 6. _____ | Wednesday | 7. _____ |

Part 2: Listening
Listen and circle the word.

1. Sunday   (Saturday)   Monday   Wednesday
2. Monday   Tuesday   Saturday   Friday
3. 6:25   6:15   7:15   6:00
4. She's sick. She's fine.   He's sick. He's fine.
5. ear   hair   arm   leg
6. headache   stomachache   earache   backache

English—No Problem! **Literacy**

Master 28b

Name:_____ Date:_____ Class:_____

Part 3: Language
Write.

I'm	It's	She's	✔ He's	It's	He's

1. How's your husband? ____He's____ fine.
2. What day is today? _____ Tuesday.
3. What time is it? _____ 3:30.
4. How is your daughter? _____ fine.
5. How is your son? _____ sick.
6. How are you? _____ fine.

Part 4: Vocabulary
Write.

arm	stomachache	hand	headache	leg	✔ nose

1. ____nose____
2. _____
3. _____
4. _____
5. _____
6. _____

English—No Problem! **Literacy**

Master 29   Use after Lesson 1, page 55.

Name: _____ Date: _____ Class: _____

Unit 4: Money! Money! Money!
Game: Spend! Spend! Spend!

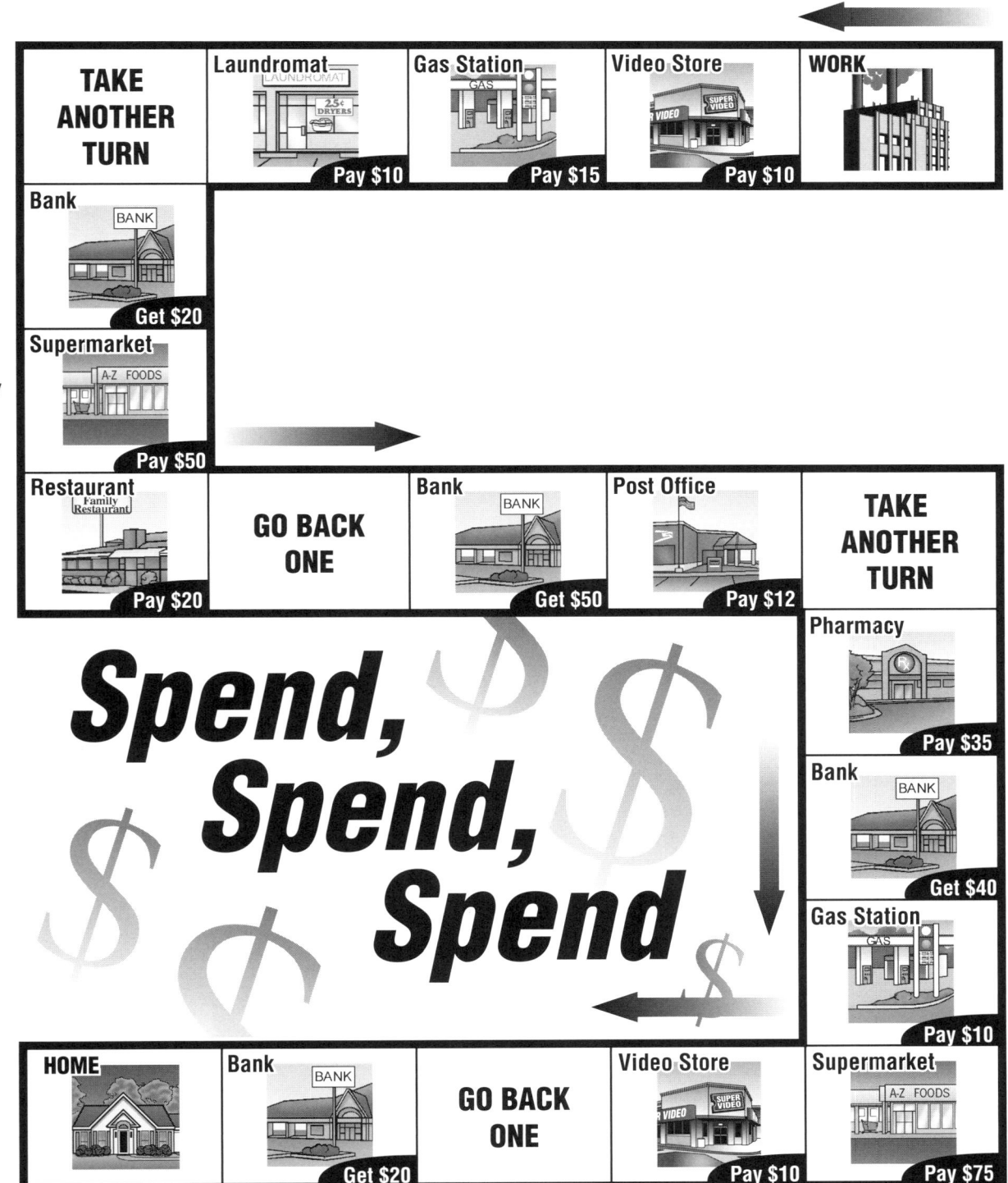

Count your money! The winner has the most money.

Master 30   Use after Lesson 1, page 56.

Name: _____ Date: _____ Class: _____

Unit 4: Money! Money! Money!
Reading: The Letter T

A. Copy T and t.

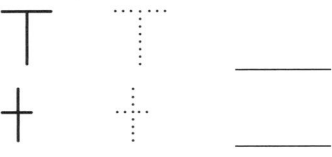

B. Listen and write.

to	__o	_____
ten	__en	_____
two	__wo	_____
twenty	__wenty	_____
Tuesday	__uesday	_____
Tony	__ony	_____

C. Write more words with t. Copy the words.

1. repea__t__   ____repeat____
2. i__   _____
3. las__   _____
4. firs__   _____
5. poin__   _____
6. foo__   _____
7. amoun__   _____
8. eigh__   _____

English—No Problem!   **Literacy**

Master 31 Use after Lesson 2, page 58.

Name:_____ Date:_____ Class:_____

Unit 4: Money! Money! Money!
Reading: Months

Cut out the letters. Use them to spell the 12 months.

a	a	a	a	A	a	A
b	b	b	b	b	c	c
c	D	e	e	e	e	e
e	e	e	e	e	e	F
g	h	i	J	J	J	l
l	M	M	m	m	m	n
n	N	O	o	o	p	p
r	r	r	r	r	r	r
r	r	s	S	t	t	t
u	u	u	u	u	u	v
y	y	y	y			

English—No Problem! **Literacy**

Master 32 Use after Lesson 2, page 59.

Name: _____ Date: _____ Class: _____

Unit 4: Money, Money, Money!
Life Skills: Writing a Check

Partner A — *speaks.*

Date: October 20, 2005
Amount: $35.15
Pay to: Cool Light Electric
Signature: Luis DeFaz

Partner A — *writes.*

```
Luis DeFaz                                      1632
54 North Ave.
West Beach, CA 92001

PAY TO THE
ORDER OF _____   $ [     ]

_____ DOLLARS

First Bank
Los Angeles, CA 92005

MEMO _____

⑆ 983042999 ⑆   7854  00310 ⑈  1632
```

fold line here

Partner B — *speaks.*

Date: February 16, 2006
Amount: $135.87
Pay to: Hot Times Gas Company
Signature: Marisol Osario

Partner B — *writes.*

```
Marisol Osario                                   345
1220 W. Elm St.
West Beach, CA 92001

PAY TO THE
ORDER OF _____   $ [     ]

_____ DOLLARS

Union Bank

MEMO _____

⑆ 222271346 ⑆   4672  92677 ⑈ 2 ⑈  0345
```

English—No Problem! **Literacy**

Master 33 Use after Lesson 2, page 60.

Name:_____ Date:_____ Class:_____

Unit 4: Money! Money! Money!
Reading: The Letter F

A. Copy F and f.

F F ____
f f ____

B. Listen and write.

for   __or   _____

form   __orm   _____

fever   __ever   _____

first   __irst   _____

family   __amily   _____

February __ebruary _____

Friday   __riday   _____

C. Write more words with f. Copy the words.

1. fi_f_teen   ____fifteen____

2. fi__ty   _____

3. wi__e   _____

4. grand__ather   _____

5. o__fice   _____

6. hal__   _____

English—No Problem! **Literacy**

Master 34   Use with the Unit 4 Project, page 61.

Name: _____   Date: _____   Class: _____

Unit 4: Money, Money, Money!
Unit 4 Project: Places You Pay Cash

Get in a group. Assign a writer, timekeeper, reporter, and materials leader. The materials leader is the person who will get the handout and scissors and cut things out.

1. Write the names.

Writer _____   Timekeeper _____

Reporter _____   Materials Leader _____

2. Talk about the pictures. Ask and answer questions about the pictures.
Do you pay cash at the gas station? __Yes, Jose pays cash__.

3. Write a list of places people pay cash.

4. Report to the class. Listen and check the places on your list.

One Step Up
Write sentences about the class.

_____ students pay cash at the _____.

_____ students pay cash at the _____.

_____ students pay cash at the _____.

English—No Problem! Literacy

Master 35a Use to assess or review Unit 4.

Name: _____ Date: _____ Class: _____

Unit 4: Money, Money, Money!
Unit Checkup/Review

Part 1: Learning for Life
Write a check.

```
Armando Diaz                                              8832
1234 Black Street
Cambridge, MA 02139      ②_____ _____

PAY TO THE  ⑤                                    $  [        ] ④
ORDER OF _____
⑥ _____ DOLLARS
Savings Bank
1657 Norfolk St.
Cambridge, MA 02139
MEMO ①  For Electric Bill      ③ _____
⑆:07798 261⑆: 4500033221 ⑆ 8832
```

1. For: electric bill
2. Date: October 23, 2005
3. signature: Armando Diaz
4. amount in numbers: $78.65
5. pay to: Power and Light Company
6. amount in words: Seventy-eight and 65/100

Part 2: Listening
Listen. Circle.

1. He's at	the supermarket.	work.	(the bank.)
2. I need change for a	hundred.	ten.	twenty.
3. Yes, I have	four dollars.	four quarters.	four dimes.
4. It's	11/5.	6/3.	4/12.
5. April is	M-A-R-C-H.	A-P-R-I-L.	J-U-L-Y.
6. I need to cash a	coin.	change.	check.

English—No Problem! **Literacy**

Master 35b

Name: _____ Date: _____ Class: _____

Part 3: Language

Write.

1. pay? / you / do / How   _How do you pay?_

2. name? / What's / your   _____

3. birthday? / is / your / When   _____

4. cash? / you / do / Where / pay   _____

Answer the questions.

5. What's your name? _____

6. When is your birthday? _____

Part 4: Vocabulary

Write numbers.

1. five dollars and 25 cents   _$5.25_

2. fifty cents   _____

3. twenty-eight dollars and seventy cents   _____

Write words.

4. 9/15/05   _September 15, 2005_

5. 4/16/07   _____

6. 7/4/05   _____

7. 2/14/08   _____

English—No Problem! Literacy

Master 36   Use after Lesson 1, page 65.

Name: _____ Date: _____ Class: _____

Unit 5: No Milk
Life Skills: Organize Information

| bananas | ✔chicken | potatoes | oranges | shrimp |
| apples | fish | tomatoes | beef | carrots |

A. Write the words under the correct word.

Meat
chicken
_____

_____

Seafood
_____

_____

Vegetables
_____

_____

_____

Fruit
_____

_____

_____

B. Now write the words in alphabetical order.

Meat
1. _beef_
2. _____

Seafood
6. _____
7. _____

Vegetables
3. _____
4. _____
5. _____

Fruit
8. _____
9. _____
10. _____

English—No Problem! **Literacy**

Master 37   Use after Lesson 1, page 65.

Name: _____ Date: _____ Class: _____

Unit 5: No Milk
Reading: The Letter *H*

A. Copy *H* and *h*.

H   H   ____
h   h   ____

B. Listen and write.

he	__e	_____
half	__alf	_____
hand	__and	_____
head	__ead	_____
home	__ome	_____
hospital	__ospital	_____
hundred	__undred	_____

C. Write more words with *h*. Copy the words.

1. _h_ eadac _h_ e   _headache_
2. backac__e   _____
3. t__ree   _____
4. fis__   _____
5. c__icken   _____
6. s__rimp   _____
7. eig__t   _____
8. Marc__   _____

English—No Problem! Literacy

Master 38   Use after Lesson 2, page 68.

Name:_____ Date:_____ Class:_____

Unit 5: No Milk
Game: Match the Facts

Work with a partner. Pick up a problem. Do you have the answer?
If you do, put the answer with the problem.

Problems

$80.00 +20.00	$46.00 + 3.00	$35.00 +25.00	$56.40 +13.10
$61.30 +27.20	$25.50 + 2.50	$54.00 − 3.00	$89.00 − 63.00
$66.50 − 24.50	$55.50 − 36.50	$95.50 − 17.25	$78.25 − 17.25

Answers

$28.00	$49.00	$100.00
$60.00	$69.50	$88.50
$51.00	$42.00	$26.00
$78.25	$61.00	$19.00

English—No Problem! Literacy

Master 39 Use after Lesson 2, page 70.

Name: _____ Date: _____ Class: _____

Unit 5: No Milk
Reading: The Letter L

A. Copy L and l.

L L ____

l l ____

B. Listen and write.

leg	__eg	_____
last	__ast	_____
list	__ist	_____
like	__ike	_____
less	__ess	_____
laundromat	__aundromat	_____
Lela	__e__a	_____

C. Write more words with l. Copy the words.

1. cerea__l__   ____cereal____
2. schoo__   _____
3. spel__   _____
4. bi__ __   _____
5. nicke__   _____
6. dol__ar   _____
7. ha__f   _____
8. midd__e   _____

English—No Problem! Literacy

Master 40

Use with the Unit 5 Project, page 71.

Name: _____ Date: _____ Class: _____

Unit 5: No Milk
Unit 5 Project: Going Shopping

Write the names of supermarkets. Then write the addresses.
Write the prices of the foods.

Supermarket	Address						

Finished? Show this to the class and talk about the prices.

English—No Problem! **Literacy**

Master 41a Use to assess or review Unit 5.

Name: _____ Date: _____ Class: _____

Unit 5: No Milk
Unit Checkup/Review

Part 1: Learning for Life

   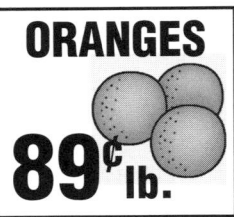 

1. How many pounds is a bag of potatoes? ____5 pounds____

2. How many pounds is a basket of tomatoes? _____

3. How much are apples? _____ 4. Oranges? _____

5. What costs less, the bread or the potatoes? _____

6. What costs less, the apples or the oranges? _____

Part 2: Listening
Listen. Circle.

1. (a. bread)   b. noodles   c. rice   d. milk
2. a. potatoes   b. carrots   c. tomatoes   d. oranges
3. a. oil   b. tea   c. water   d. coffee
4. a. apples   b. bananas   c. carrots   d. oranges
5. a.    b.    c.    d.
6. a.  b.  c.   d.

English—No Problem! Literacy

Master 4Ib

Name: _____ Date: _____ Class: _____

Part 3: Language
Write.

| bananas | chicken | potatoes | oranges | shrimp |
| apples | ✔fish | tomatoes | beef | carrots |

1. For dinner, I like _____fish_____.
2. For breakfast, I like _____.
3. For lunch, I like _____.

Write three foods you need at home.

4. _I need chicken._____
5. _____
6. _____
7. _____

Part 4: Vocabulary
Write the words.

| apples | ✔beef | carrots | chicken | juice |
| milk | oranges | potatoes | ✔bananas | water |

Meat
1. ___beef___
2. _____

Drinks
3. _____
4. _____
5. _____

Vegetables
6. _____
7. _____

Fruits
8. ___bananas___
9. _____
10. _____

English—No Problem! Literacy

Master 42   Use after Lesson 2, page 79.

Name: _____ Date: _____ Class: _____

Unit 6: Hurry Up!
Reading: The Letter S

A. Copy *S* and *s*.

S   S   _____

s   s   _____

B. Listen and write.

snowy	__nowy	_____
sunny	__unny	_____
shorts	__hort__	_____
sunglasses	__ungla__ __e__	_____
boots	boot__	_____
bus	bu__	_____
signs	__ign__	_____

C. Write more words with *s*. Copy the words.

1. j <u>e</u> <u>a</u> <u>n</u> <u>s</u>
   _____jeans_____

2. s__ __r__s
   _____

3. sc__ __ __ __
   _____

4. __t __p
   _____

5. h__s__ __t__ __
   _____

6. __t__ __i__ __
   _____

Show the words to your teacher. Show the words to a classmate.

English—No Problem! Literacy

Master 43 Use after Lesson 2, page 79.

Name:_____ Date:_____ Class:_____

Unit 6: Hurry Up!
Reading: The Letter R

A. Copy R and r.

R R ____

r r ____

B. Listen and write.

rainy   __ainy   _____

read   __ead   _____

rice   __ice   _____

repeat   __epeat   _____

ride   __ide   _____

railroad __ailroad _____

Ron   __on   _____

C. Write more words with r. Copy the words.

1. sweate_r_   _sweater_   6. qua__te__   _____
2. mothe__   _____   7. weathe__   _____
3. wa__m   _____   8. o__de__   _____
4. ski__t   _____   9. b__othe__   _____
5. fathe__   _____   10. siste__   _____

English—No Problem! **Literacy**

Master 44   Use after Lesson 2, page 79.

Name:_____ Date:_____ Class:_____

Unit 6: Hurry Up!
Life Skills: Organize Information

Look. Write.

1. _____

2. _____

3. _____

4. _____

5. _____

6. _____

7. _____

8. _____

9. _____

10. _____

weather   **clothing**   **places**

__rainy__   _____   _____

_____   _____   _____

_____   _____   _____

                 _____

English—No Problem!   **Literacy**

Master 45   Use after Lesson 2, page 79.

Name:_____ Date:_____ Class:_____

Unit 6: Hurry Up!
Game: Match the Words

Column 1	Column 2
hot	90°+
cold	0°– 39°
warm	70°– 89°
cool	40°– 69°
umbrella	rainy
boots	snowy
sunglasses	sunny
coat	cold
drive	a car
take	a bus
ride	a bicycle
bus	stop
train	station
police	department

Read and say the words to your teacher.

English—No Problem!   Literacy

Master 46   Use with the Unit 6 Project, page 81.

Name: _____ Date: _____ Class: _____

Unit 6: Hurry Up!
Unit 6 Project: Make a Class Map

A. Write the names of students in your group.

_____   _____

_____   _____

_____   _____

B. Write addresses of students.

Name	Address
_____	_____
_____	_____
_____	_____
_____	_____
_____	_____
_____	_____

C. Write about a place in your community.

The address for _____ is _____

_____.

The phone number for _____ is _____.

English—No Problem!   **Literacy**

Master 47a Use to assess or review Unit 6.

Name: _____ Date: _____ Class: _____

Unit 6: Hurry Up!
Unit Checkup/Review

Part 1: Learning for Life
Write the weather.

Wednesday   Thursday   Friday   Saturday   Sunday

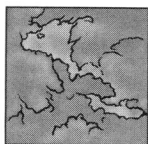  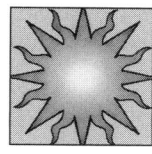  

1. Friday ___sunny___   3. Thursday _____

2. Sunday _____   4. Saturday _____

5. What's the weather today? _____

Part 2: Listening
Listen and circle.

1. It's rainy.   (It's windy.)   It's cloudy.
2. No, it isn't.   Yes, I do.   It sure is!
3. Yes, I do.   No, I don't.   No, I do.
4. It's 19°.   It's 90°.   It's 99°.

Part 3: Language
Answer yes or no.

1. Do you have an umbrella? ___Yes, I do._____

2. Do you walk to school? _____

3. Do you drive to school? _____

4. Do you work? _____

GO ON

English—No Problem! **Literacy**

Master 47b

Name: _____ Date: _____ Class: _____

Part 4: Vocabulary

Match.

Write.

1.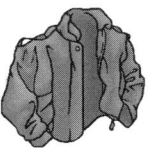
   skirt
   gloves
   jeans

7.  ___train station___

2.
   shorts
   sunglasses
   sweater

8. 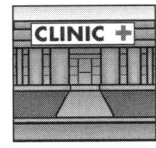 _____

3.
   jeans
   sweater
   jacket

9.  _____

4.
   shirt
   skirt
   shorts

10.  _____

5.
   raincoat
   umbrella
   boots

11. _____

6.
   coat
   skirt
   jeans

12. _____

English—No Problem! Literacy

Answers and Listening Scripts

English Beginnings A: Cecile's Day
Master 9 Reading: Letters and Numbers

	5	6	7	8
C	C	H	A	T
D	T	A	S	K

	1	2	3	4
A	R	E	A	D
B	C	O	P	Y

English Beginnings B: Omar's Day
Master 11 Reading: Find the Letter

Partner B follows directions.

2. C(e)cil(e)
3. alp(h)abet
4. parking l(o)t
5. of(f)ice
6. ho(m)e
7. li(s)ten
8. pharmac(y)

Partner A follows directions.

2. r(e)ad
3. v(i)deo
4. sto(r)e
5. whi(t)e
6. oran(g)e
7. eig(h)t
8. (z)ero

Master 15 Listening Script

A Number one, check.
Number two, learn.
Number three, read.
Number four, write.
Number five, point.
Number six, listen.
Number seven, repeat.
Number eight, speak.

B Number twelve, notebook.
Number thirteen, pen.
Number fourteen, book.
Number fifteen, home.
Number sixteen, classroom.
Number seventeen, teacher.
Number eighteen, pencil.
Number nineteen, student.

Unit 1 Checkup/Review
Master 17 Listening Script

1. Teacher: How many pencils are there?
   Student: Eleven pencils.
2. Student: Is this a classroom?
   Teacher: No, it's an office.
   Student: What?
   Teacher: An office.
3. Teacher: Class, look at the board.
   Student: Excuse me?
   Teacher: Look.
4. Teacher: Read the book, Marina.
   Student: OK.
   Teacher: Read.
5. Teacher: You're in classroom number 4.
   Student: What?
   Teacher: Your classroom—it's number 4.
6. Student: We need fourteen books.
   Teacher: How many books?

Student: Fourteen books.

Answers

Part 1 (5 points each)
2, 3. Answers will vary.
5. twelve and 00/100
6. eleven and 00/100
7. sixteen and 00/100

Part 2 (5 points each)
2. an office
3. look
4. read
5. classroom
6. fourteen books

Part 3 (5 points each)
2. pens
3. school
4. notebooks
5. teacher

Part 4 (5 points each)
2. speak
3. *read* checked
4. *school* circled
5. listen
6. *office* checked
7. *classroom* circled

Unit 2 Checkup/Review
Master 22 Listening Script

1. Ina: Who's that?
   Louise: That's my mother.
2. Ina: Who's that?
   Louise: That's my daughter, Veronica.
3. Louise: Who's that?
   Ina: That's my son, Victor.
4. Raul: Who's that?
   Mark: That's my wife, Susana.
5. Mark: Who's that?
   Raul: That's my grandson, Philip.
6. Mark: Who's that?
   Louise: That's my grandfather.

Answers

Part 1 (5 points each)
2. 42-09-7-18
3. 2592 Purple St.
4. 60126
5. 773-555-9287
6. IL

Part 2 (5 points each)
2. daughter
3. son
4. wife
5. grandson
6. grandfather

Part 3 (5 points each)
2. he
3. she
4. you
5. they

Part 4 (5 points each)
2. 22
3. 30
4. 28
6. He is a husband.
7. She is a daughter.
8. They are women.

Unit 3: You're Sick!
Master 26 Life Skills: Using Polite Language

Dialogue A
1: Your son is sick.
2: What's wrong?
1: He has a stomachache.
2: Could you repeat that?
1: A stomachache. He has a stomachache.

Dialogue B

1: I can't go to work Thursday.
2: Excuse me. Tuesday?
1: No. Thursday.
2: Oh. OK. See you Friday.

Unit 3 Checkup/Review
Master 28 Listening Script

1. Dan: What day is today?
   Lu: It's Saturday!
2. Lu: Is today Thursday?
   Dan: No, it's Friday.
3. Lu: Is it 6:30 yet?
   Dan: No, it's just 6:15.
4. Lu: How's your son?
   Dan: He's sick.
5. Lu: What's wrong?
   Dan: It's his ear.
6. Dan: He has an earache.

Answers

Part 1 (5 points each)
2. It's 2:00.
3. It's 9:15.
4. It's 10:45.
6. Tuesday
7. Thursday

Part 2 (5 points each)
2. Friday
3. 6:15
4. He's sick.
5. ear
6. earache

Part 3 (5 points each)
2. It's Tuesday.
3. It's 3:30.
4. She's fine.
5. He's sick.
6. I'm fine.

Part 4 (5 points each)
2. arm
3. hand
4. leg
5. headache
6. stomachache

Unit 4: Money, Money, Money!
Master 31 Reading: Months

January
February
March
April
May
June
July
August
September
October
November
December

Master 32 Life Skills: Writing a Check

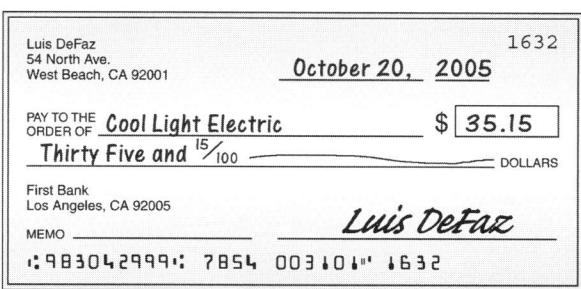

Unit 4 Checkup/Review
Master 35 Listening Script

1. Sophia: Where's Armando?
   Hal: He's at the bank.
2. Hal: Can I help you?
   Sophia: I need change for a hundred.
3. Hal: Do you have change for a dollar?
   Sophia: Let me see. Yes, I have four quarters.
4. Sophia: What's the date?
   Hal: It's June third.
5. Hal: How do you spell April?
   Sophia: April is A-P-R-I-L.
6. Sophia: Where are you going?
   Hal: To the bank. I need to cash a check.

Answers

Part 1 (5 points each)

```
Armando Diaz                                    8832
1234 Black Street
Cambridge, MA 02139      October 23    2005

PAY TO THE
ORDER OF  Power and Light Company    $ 78.65
Seventy-eight and 65/100                DOLLARS
Savings Bank
1657 Norfolk St.
Cambridge, MA 02139
MEMO    For Electric Bill        Armando Diaz
⑈07798 261⑈ 4500033221  8832
```

Part 2 (5 points each)

2. hundred
3. four quarters
4. 6/3
5. A-P-R-I-L
6. check

Part 3 (5 points each)

2. What's your name?
3. When is your birthday?
4. Where do you pay cash?
5. Answers will vary.
6. Answers will vary.

Part 4 (5 points each)

2. $.50
3. $28.70

5. April 16, 2007
6. July 4, 2005
7. February 14, 2008

Unit 5: No Milk!
Master 36 Life Skills: Organize Information

A. | Meat | Vegetables | Seafood | Fruit |
|---|---|---|---|
| chicken | potatoes | shrimp | bananas |
| beef | tomatoes | fish | apples |
| | carrots | | oranges |

B. | Meat | Vegetables | Seafood | Fruit |
|---|---|---|---|
| 1. beef | 3. carrots | 6. fish | 8. apples |
| 2. chicken | 4. potatoes | 7. shrimp | 9. bananas |
| | 5. tomatoes | | 10. oranges |

Master 38 Game: Match the Facts

$80.00
+20.00
$100.00

$61.30
+27.20
$88.50

$66.50
- 24.50
$42.00

$46.00
+ 3.00
$49.00

$25.50
+ 2.50
$28.00

$55.50
- 36.50
$19.00

$35.00
+25.00
$60.00

$54.00
- 3.00
$51.00

$95.50
- 17.25
$78.25

$56.40
+13.10
$69.50

$89.00
- 63.00
$26.00

$78.25
- 17.25
$61.00

Unit 5 Checkup/Review
Master 41 Listening Script

1. An: Do we have bread?
   Cam: No, we don't have any bread.
   An: I'll buy some.
2. Cam: Can you buy some tomatoes?
   An: What?
   Cam: Some tomatoes. Buy some tomatoes.
3. An: When you go to the store, please pick up some coffee.
   Cam: A pound of coffee?
   An: No, buy two pounds of coffee.
4. Cam: Honey, can you help me with the grocery list?
   An: Sure. Do we need carrots?
   Cam: Yes, we do. Carrots.
5. Cam: Honey, can you help me with the grocery list?
   An: Okay. I think we need noodles.
   Cam: We *do* need noodles.
6. An: Are you going to the store?
   Cam: Yes.
   An: Buy some chicken for dinner.

Answers

Part 1 (5 points each)
2. 2 pounds
3. $.59/lb.
4. $.89/lb.
5. bread
6. apples

Part 2 (5 points each)
2. c. tomatoes
3. d. coffee
4. c. carrots
5. b. noodles
6. d. chicken

Part 3 (2, 3 – 4 points each; 5, 6, 7 – 6 points each)
Answers will vary.

Part 4 (3 points each)
Order may vary.
Meat: chicken, beef
Drinks: juice, milk, water
Vegetables: carrots, potatoes
Fruit: apples, bananas, oranges

English—No Problem! **Literacy 63**

Unit 6: Hurry Up!
Master 42 Reading: The Letter *S*

C. 2. shorts 4. stop 6. station
   3. school 5. hospital

Master 44 Life Skills: Organize Information

1. train station
2. skirt
3. sweater
4. coat
5. jeans
6. police department
7. rainy
8. school
9. snowy
10. sunny

Weather	Clothing	Places
rainy	jeans	train station
snowy	skirt	police department
sunny	sweater	school
	coat	

Master 45 Game: Match the Words

hot, 90°+
cold, 0°–39°
warm, 70°–89°
cool, 40°–69°
umbrella, rainy
boots, snowy
sunglasses, sunny
coat, cold
drive, a car
take, a bus
ride, a bicycle
bus, stop
train, station
police, department

Unit 6 Checkup/Review
Master 47 Listening Script

1. Rose: How's the weather?
   Jake: It's windy.
2. Jake: It's a nice day.
   Rose: It sure is!
3. Rose: Do you have my umbrella?
   Jake: No, I don't.
4. Jake: What's the temperature for tomorrow?
   Rose: 90 degrees.

Answers

Part 1 (5 points each)
2. windy
3. rainy
4. snowy
5. Answers may vary.

Part 2 (5 points each)
2. It sure is!
3. No, I don't.
4. 90 degrees

Part 3 (5 points each)
2–5 Yes, I do. OR No, I don't. for each.

Part 4 (5 points each)
2. sweater
3. jacket
4. shirt
5. boots
6. jeans
8. school
9. railroad crossing
10. clinic
11. bus stop
12. stop